Is socialist revolution in the US possible?

Is socialist revolution in the US possible?

A NECESSARY DEBATE
AMONG WORKING PEOPLE

MARY-ALICE WATERS

PATHFINDER
NEW YORK   LONDON   MONTREAL   SYDNEY

ISBN 978-1-60488-090-8
Library of Congress Control Number 2016953168

Manufactured in the United States of America

First edition, 2008
Second edition, 2009
Third edition, 2016

COVER DESIGN: Toni Gorton

COVER PAINTING: Helen Frankenthaler, *Sandstorm*, 1992, acrylic on canvas, 50 x 91⅜ inches. © 2016 Helen Frankenthaler Foundation, Inc. / Artists Rights Society (ARS), New York.

PATHFINDER
www.pathfinderpress.com
E-mail: pathfinder@pathfinderpress.com

CONTENTS

About the authors   7

Preface to the third edition
Norton Sandler   9

Introduction
Norton Sandler   15

Is socialist revolution in the US possible?
Mary-Alice Waters   29

'The class battles ahead are inevitable, their outcome
is not. That depends on us.'
Mary-Alice Waters   53

Prospects for revolution in the US
A necessary debate among working people
Olympia Newton   65

Index   83

ABOUT THE AUTHORS

MARY-ALICE WATERS is a member of the Socialist Workers Party National Committee. She is editor of *New International* magazine and president of Pathfinder Press. Waters is editor of Pathfinder's series of more than two dozen books on the Cuban Revolution in world politics. *Rosa Luxemburg Speaks*; *Malcolm X, Black Liberation, and the Road to Workers Power*; *Cosmetics, Fashions, and the Exploitation of Women;* and *Voices from Prison: The Cuban Five* are among the numerous other Pathfinder titles she has edited and contributed to.

NORTON SANDLER is a member of the Socialist Workers Party National Committee as well as a longtime leader of the party's trade union work.

OLYMPIA NEWTON, a *Militant* staff member and leader of the Young Socialists in the United States, covered the 2007 Venezuela International Book Fair for the socialist newsweekly, which is published in New York.

Preface to the third edition

NORTON SANDLER

Is Socialist Revolution in the US Possible? The answer given here by Mary-Alice Waters is an unequivocal, "Yes!"

That is, however, only the first of the important questions addressed during what became the deepgoing international debate recorded in these pages. Even if a socialist revolution is possible, is it *"necessary"*? Why can't capitalism be "regulated" and made to serve the interests of the overwhelming majority of humanity? What does the oft-abused term "revolution" mean? And are there any living examples we can learn from?

This 2016 edition of *Is Socialist Revolution in the US Possible?* appears some eight years after the near meltdown of the world capitalist banking system in the closing months of 2008. That financial and stock market panic soon exposed a far deeper underlying crisis: the long downward trend of capitalist profit rates in the United States and internationally, and the resulting contraction of investment in production, trade, and hiring. A slow-burning worldwide depression had begun.

Despite assurances by high-ranking public officials, including President Barack Obama, that the US economy has now "recovered" from the worst financial crisis since the 1930s and is doing "pretty darn well," working people know in our bones that for us it's a lie. A lie borne out by the facts we live with.

Median household income is today more than $4,000 lower than it was in 1999, seventeen years ago, and that is often the cumulative income from multiple jobs worked by everyone in the family who can become a wage earner. The labor force participation rate (the size of the "working class" as measured by the capitalist government) is lower than any time since 1978, largely because more and more workers haven't been able to find a job and aren't currently looking.

Inflation, they tell us, is basically flat, but just since the turn of the century rents have more than doubled on average, as have school fees and childcare, while medical costs and the hit at the grocery store have gone up nearly 100 percent. In the last year alone, health insurance jumped on average by 7 percent, school lunches by nearly 6 percent, and transit fares by more than 5 percent.

Afghanistan, Iraq, Syria, Libya—Washington's wars and their grisly consequences at home and around the world keep metastasizing. Tens of millions are homeless and displaced.

The presumption of stability and a new era of peace and prosperity born of an "ever closer" European Union has shattered. The economic social and political crises in Latin America, Africa, and Asia are deepening.

Told they have to choose between two of the most broadly distrusted presidential candidates in US history, is it any surprise so many answer, "I won't happily vote for either one!"

This 2016 edition of *Is Socialist Revolution in the US Possible?* is addressed to working people—in city, town, and countryside—across the US and around the world, who are searching for proletarian solidarity and a way forward in this world of deepening capitalist conflict. It is addressed to the women and men of every skin color, religion, national origin, and age who are every day more determined to understand the roots of what is happening to their families and themselves, more open to joining together with others to fight for a future only we can create.

◆

The five-day rolling political debate on which this book is based took place in November 2007 at the Venezuela International Book Fair, a popular cultural festival held yearly in Caracas. The book centers around the talk given by Mary-Alice Waters, a leader of the Socialist Workers Party in the US and president of Pathfinder Press, who opened the panel discussion on "The United States: A Possible Revolution," the book fair's theme. The narrative is driven forward by the responses and reactions to the issues posed by Waters, as well as her answers.

The wide-ranging debate that unfolded was unique in its depth and clarity. Although virtually all twenty-two panelists were from the US, certainly no similar exchange among the different political currents they represented has taken place in living memory.

Is the integration of millions of toilers from Latin America and around the world into the US working class a potential strength or fatal source of weakness and division? Are US workers so corrupted by the wealth of US capitalist society that they are incapable of revolutionary struggle? Were the American War of Independence from the British crown and the US Civil War the First and Second American Revolutions, or has there never been a revolutionary struggle of any kind in US history? Has "white skin privilege" destroyed every progressive social struggle in US history? Do Jews control the banks and capitalist media conglomerates of the world? Was 9/11 an Israeli conspiracy? Does Cuba remain the only "free territory of the Americas," or is Venezuela showing the toilers of the world a new road to socialism?

These were among the sharply counterposed perspectives on fundamental questions of revolutionary strategy and perspectives presented and debated with only a few breaches of civility.

Waters's presentation appears here along with an introduction summarizing the issues that were joined. An article by staff writer Olympia Newton from the pages of the *Militant* newspaper reports on the political exchange, which involved several hundred audience participants in addition to the panelists.

When the November 2007 debate took place, only the first tremors of the coming housing-fueled "debt crisis" and subsequent near-collapse of the credit and banking system had been felt.

One year later, the dam had burst, and the consequences were beginning to be felt by working people the world over. At the November 2008 Caracas book fair—on the first anniversary of the exchange—Monte Ávila, one of Venezuela's leading publishers, presented an edition of *Is Socialist Revolution in the US Possible?* for sale in bookstores throughout that country. They also distributed a thousand copies of a special printing without charge to young readers at the fair.

Speaking at the Caracas launching of the Monte Ávila edition, Waters described what had transpired the previous twelve months. She looked back at the debate that had taken place a year earlier in light of the economic and social crisis, which was rapidly escalating and expanding geographically, including across Latin America.

This 2016 edition of *Is Socialist Revolution in the US Possible?*, like the second edition published in 2009, includes both talks by Waters.

Readers will judge for themselves how well the perspectives laid out almost a decade ago have stood the test of time.

SEPTEMBER 2016

Introduction

BY NORTON SANDLER

THE CENTRAL POLITICAL EVENT of the 2007 Venezuela International Book Fair held in Caracas was a five-day rolling exchange on the topic "The United States: A Possible Revolution."

The timely initiative by Venezuela's National Book Center opened discussion "on a question the answer to which, in practice, will ultimately determine the future of humanity—or more accurately perhaps, whether there *is* a future for humanity," said Mary-Alice Waters in her remarks kicking off what became a wide-ranging debate.

This small book contains the opening presentation by Waters, as well as coverage of the lively multiday forum from the pages of the US socialist newsweekly, the *Militant*. Waters, a member of the Socialist Workers Party National Committee and president of Pathfinder Press, edited and wrote the preface to Pathfinder's *Cuba and the Coming American Revolution* by Jack Barnes, which she drew on in her remarks. The book—among the titles recently issued in Venezuela by Monte Ávila, one of that country's leading publishers—was presented at the fair in meetings sponsored both by Monte Ávila and by Pathfinder.

Some twenty-two participants addressed the November 10–14 activity widely publicized as the "central forum" of the book fair. Almost all had long been involved in various social protest movements and political parties in the United States. Several currently live in Venezuela, but the majority traveled from North America to take part in the book fair. Widely diverging and often sharply counterposed views were aired in the course of what was, with one notable exception, a model of civil debate for the workers movement. The exchange achieved an unusual degree of clarity on conflicting positions advanced on a number of political issues.

The resolution of those questions, in the course of far-reaching class struggle, will decide whether the working class in the United States will transform itself into a class with a mass vanguard able to politically lead broad layers of oppressed and exploited toilers in struggles to defend their own interests.

Most sessions of the five-day activity were attended by 125 to 150 participants, and covered in Venezuelan newspapers as well as on radio and television programs carried throughout the Caribbean and South America. Olympia Newton's two-part article for the *Militant* newspaper, included here, reports on the rich debate as it unfolded around five central questions.

What prompted Pathfinder to produce this book is the importance of the issues addressed.

1. The significance of a historic new wave of immigration to the United States

Over the last two decades, millions of workers from across the Americas and the world have been brought into the mines, factories, fields, and service industries in the United

States. This has strengthened the resistance and combativity of toilers in face of the bosses' quarter-century-plus drive to brutally intensify production line speeds, lengthen the workday, and slash wages as well as health and retirement benefits.

This immigration is politicizing a layer of US workers, said Waters, who had been asked by book fair organizers to lead off the panel the opening day. She pointed to the millions who poured into the streets across the country on May Day in 2006 and 2007, taking the US rulers by surprise. That "historic working-class holiday is being reborn in the United States as a day of *struggle*," she said.

The US working class, "including its immigrant component—some twelve million of whom today carry documents not accepted by the cops and courts," Waters said, is "the source of the capitalists' surplus value, which in turn is the source of their profits, wealth, social status, and state power. They utterly depend on this massive pool of exploited and superexploited labor. They cannot compete worldwide and accumulate capital without it—and increasingly, even with it."

That's why "the battle to win the labor movement and the big majority of working people to defend the rights of immigrants is inseparable from the battle to organize the working class as a whole and rebuild the trade unions. For that reason, it has become one of the most important 'domestic' political questions in the United States today," Waters said. "Right now, it is one of the greatest obstacles to taking even baby steps toward independent working-class political action and the transformation of the unions into instruments of conscious class struggle."

This perspective, and a course of action for the working-class vanguard consistent with it, was sharply rejected by several panelists as well as by others in the audience. Speaking immediately after Waters, Venezuelan American lawyer and journalist Eva Golinger spelled out a counterposed view. Far from taking a vanguard place in growing resistance to the employers' accelerated exploitation, Golinger said, immigrant workers in the United States simply want to live in "a capitalist consumer society" and get a piece of the pie for themselves. They believe what Fox News and CNN tell them, she added.

"People are not poor or hungry in the US like they were in Venezuela," she argued. "There is poverty but only in a few small sectors. You get two or three credit cards in the mail every day." She didn't mention, of course, that if you use them you'll be even poorer and deeper in debt. Golinger said she didn't share Waters's "optimism that a revolution is possible in the United States."

A number of other speakers over the five days expressed similar contempt for the tens of millions of toilers of the Americas, Africa, and Asia driven—by the economic realities of imperialist domination in their homelands, and what they hope will be an opportunity to better their own and their children's lives—to find their way to the United States or other countries. To do so, these workers often risk their lives to get into the US, to find jobs, to survive under intense exploitation, and to send a few dollars home to their families.

As Newton reports in her articles, numerous panelists, including several who had themselves emigrated to the United States, just as vigorously countered the views expressed by Golinger and others.

2. The battle to unite the working class against the divide-and-rule strategies of the capitalist class

As Waters noted, a sharpening capitalist financial and economic crisis like the one now accelerating "will intensify the battle for the political soul of the working class" in face of efforts by the employers to turn immigrants into scapegoats for mounting joblessness and worsening economic and social conditions.

Working people in the United States "face the same class enemy," Waters said, "and determined struggles on any front tend to pull workers together in face of the attempts to divide us." More than ever before in history, she emphasized, a fighting vanguard capable of leading a successful revolutionary struggle in the United States today will bring together workers regardless of skin color, national origin, religion, or sex. Each time we fight alongside each other, "it becomes harder for the bosses to pit 'us' against 'them,'" she pointed out. "It becomes more possible to see that our class interests are not the same as those of 'our' bosses, 'our' government, or 'our' two parties."

A counterview to this perspective was expressed most sharply by panelist Amiri Baraka, a US writer who has been active in Black nationalist, Maoist, and Democratic Party politics since the 1960s. Baraka argued strongly that "white privilege" has derailed all potentially revolutionary struggles in US history, including the powerful labor upsurge of the 1930s and the mass movement that brought down the institution of Jim Crow segregation in the South by the end of the 1960s. The failure of the "white left" to organize "whites" to fight "white privilege," he said, has spelled the doom of every movement for social change.

In this version of history, race-baiting rears its ugly head. "White workers" with racial prejudices become the explanation for all defeats. Missing is the responsibility borne by the US Communist Party, from the mid-1930s on, for using its influence in the labor movement to subordinate struggles by working people and the oppressed worldwide to Moscow's quest for peaceful coexistence with the imperialist rulers. In the United States that meant diverting the great social movement that grew out of the battle to organize the industrial unions, channeling it into support for the Democratic Party and the US rulers' war aims.

In her remarks, Waters had pointed out that as a result of such political misleadership, "The revolutionary potential of the great radicalization in the 1930s was squandered and diverted into support for capitalism's 'New Deal' and its inevitable successor, the 'War Deal'— culminating in the worldwide imperialist slaughter of World War II." With the collapse of Stalinist regimes in the Soviet Union and Eastern Europe in the late 1980s and early 1990s, she said, at least that "enormous political obstacle no longer stands across the road toward independent working-class political action and revolutionary socialist leadership."

In response, Baraka said he did not share the opinion expressed by some on the panel and in the audience that racial divisions could be overcome through such struggles, because "white leaders" are interested above all in protecting their privileged positions. In short, "white privilege" has been and will be more powerful than common class interests.

3. The poison of Jew-hatred and agent-baiting in the working-class and national liberation movements

Other sharp assaults against the integrity of the workers movement were confronted during the debate as well. The toxins of Jew-hatred and agent-baiting were introduced. As always, they were intertwined with attempts to explain history as the work of powerful, unknown forces conspiring against the oppressed and exploited—rather than the scientific view advanced by Marx and Engels that "the history of all hitherto existing society is the history of class struggles." That view, presented in the Communist Manifesto, is the cornerstone of the modern workers movement.

Early in the forum, a speaker who said he was visiting from Panama declared from the floor that Jews "have all the money" and control everything from the international banking system to powerful imperialist media conglomerates. In addition, "Jews" control and direct US foreign policy, especially policy toward the Middle East. This myth, infecting growing layers of middle-class liberals and radicals in the United States and other imperialist countries today, is also widely advanced throughout Latin America, including among those who identify themselves as anti-imperialists.

On the closing day of the forum, Baraka ended his presentation by reading his verse about the events of September 11, 2001, entitled "Somebody Blew Up America." That piece asks: "Who knew the World Trade Center was gonna get bombed / Who told 4000 Israeli workers at the Twin Towers / To stay home that day / Why did Sharon stay away?"

These bigoted, conspiracy-spinning allegations defy not only the facts of what happened on September 11, they conceal the plain truth of how capitalism works. Above all, they deprive working people of the knowledge and confidence that we can be the makers of history—that our own conscious, revolutionary action, and only that, can remove the capitalist ruling families from power and prevent them from blowing up the world.

Following the initial remarks in the discussion period about the rich and all-powerful Jews, I took the floor to point out that Jew-hatred remains one of the most virulent anti-working-class weapons of the ruling classes, as it has been since the birth of the modern workers movement a century and a half ago. Recalling its ghastly consequences in the hands of Germany's imperialist rulers in the 1930s and '40s, I underlined the deadly threat to the workers movement of refusing to intransigently combat any and all targeting of Jews, Latinos, Blacks, gypsies, whites, or any other national, religious or ethnic grouping.

Agent-baiting was also introduced into the debate—the glaring departure from civil discussion noted earlier—and it was answered. Baraka accused one fellow panelist of hiding that he was a "Trotskyite" and another panelist of being an "agent" (of some unnamed power) whose objective was to abet the mobilization of a reactionary student movement in the streets of Venezuela to overthrow the elected government of Hugo Chávez.

Waters replied to Baraka. Thanking book fair organizers for making possible the expression of a broad range of views, she stressed that in order for civil debate to take place, "the poison of agent- and race-baiting" must be condemned by all.

4. The history and legacy of revolutionary struggle in the United States

"There has never been a revolution in the United States, and anyone who thinks there has been is ignorant of their own history," argued British journalist Richard Gott. Even the first bourgeois-democratic revolution in North America at the end of the 1700s—which broke the imperial domination of the thirteen colonies by the British monarchy and the English landed and merchant classes—was not a revolution, Gott said. It was simply a landgrab by the US colonial bourgeoisie, a war to seize territory from Native American tribes whose interests were being defended by British troops.

Other forum participants, especially a number from Venezuela and elsewhere in Latin America, concurred with that view. Some added that the Second American Revolution, the 1861–65 US Civil War that abolished chattel slavery, had not been a revolution either, since the federal government had not from the beginning freed all slaves and mobilized them into the ranks of the Union Army.

Panelist Lee Sustar, the labor editor of *Socialist Worker*, a publication of the International Socialist Organization in the United States, put forward a different view. "The United States was created by revolution," Sustar explained. The Civil War, he stated, was the completion of the bourgeois-democratic revolution begun with the war for independence from the British crown.

Amiri Baraka agreed that the United States has already known two revolutions, but he argued sharply that the bourgeois-democratic goals of those revolutions have not yet been achieved. "The property question was settled. Chattel slavery was eliminated," Baraka said. "But the democratic revolution has never been completed." As proof of that assertion, Baraka pointed out that Blacks don't have equality. Moreover, he added, "the United States is not a democracy."

The fact that no bourgeois-democratic revolution anywhere in the world has ever brought—or ever sought to achieve—equality for the oppressed and exploited majority of working people was conveniently ignored.

Baraka was silent on the importance to working people of space to engage in political activity—that is, the democratic rights originally won in struggle by the toilers during the First American Revolution and incorporated in the US Constitution as the first ten amendments, known as the Bill of Rights. Nor did he mention the democratic conquests of the toilers as part of the Second American Revolution, paid for in rivers of blood and incorporated in the US Constitution as the Thirteenth, Fourteenth and Fifteenth Amendments.

Not only were slavery and all forms of involuntary servitude abolished with the adoption of the Thirteenth Amendment. The Fourteenth Amendment established that all persons born or naturalized in the United States are citizens, and no person subject to US jurisdiction—not just citizens or Green Card holders—can be deprived of "life, liberty, or property, without due process of law" or denied "equal protection of the laws."

The Fifteenth Amendment affirmed that the right to vote cannot be "denied or abridged" on account of "race, color, or previous condition of servitude," a victory that also paved the way for the adoption fifty years later of the Nineteenth Amendment extending the franchise to women.

"To this day democratic rights won by the toilers in revolutionary struggle remain flash points of the class struggle in the US."

Top: May 19, 1870. Six-mile long march in Baltimore, Maryland, celebrates passage of Fifteenth Amendment to the US Constitution. The right to vote "shall not be abridged or denied" on account of "race, color, or previous condition of servitude," it says.

Bottom: Exercising that right, recently enfranchised Blacks in Lincoln County, Georgia, rifles in hand, ford a creek on their way to vote.

To this day these democratic rights and their defense remain flash points of the class struggle in the US. That fact alone underscores why they are of no small consequence for working people as they take to the streets fighting for further gains.

5. Revolutionary prospects for workers and farmers in the United States

Such disputed questions of history are not arcane differences of no consequence for today. Those arguing most strongly that no revolution has ever taken place in the United States were among the most vociferous in insisting that working people in the US are incapable of revolutionary struggle now or in the future. "The only hope is Latin America," concluded Richard Gott.

Eva Golinger argued that "the only way to achieve structural change in the United States is to make advances here" in Venezuela. And, she made it clear, it is the course of Venezuela, not the example of the Cuban Revolution, that shows the way forward today.

For Amiri Baraka the conclusion was obvious too. If the bourgeois-democratic revolution was incomplete, then bourgeois reform is what's on the agenda in the United States today. He laid out his program to complete that task as part of a bloc with African American sections of the bourgeoisie. The program he spelled out was aimed not at advancing a revolutionary struggle by the working class and its allies to take state power out of the hands of the capitalist rulers. Instead, Baraka advocated rewriting the Constitution of the United States and replacing the current bicameral Congress with a unicameral parliamentary system similar to what exists in the big majority of imperialist powers.

Nothing could have been in sharper contrast to Waters's opening remarks that, "Yes, revolution *is* possible in the United States. Socialist revolution. To put it in class terms, a proletarian revolution—the broadest, most inclusive social upheaval of the oppressed and exploited imaginable, and the rebuilding of economic and social relations in their interests. . . .

"What's more, revolutionary *struggle* by the toilers along the path I just described is *inevitable*." What is not inevitable, Waters emphasized, "is the outcome of these coming revolutionary struggles. . . . That is why what we do *now*, while there is time to prepare, weighs so heavily. What kind of nucleus of what kind of revolutionary organization are we building today? What program, what continuity guides its trajectory?"

◆

These were the important issues discussed and debated during the Caracas exchange on "The United States: A Possible Revolution." And the reason this record of that debate will be of substantial interest, far beyond those who participated in it.

MARCH 2008

PHOTOS: MAGGIE TROWE/MILITANT

"The theme for this event, 'The United States: A Possible Revolution,' opens discussion on a question whose answer will determine the future of humanity."

Top: Opening day of November 2007 debate. Speaking, Mary-Alice Waters, president of Pathfinder Press. Others, left to right, are lawyer and journalist Eva Golinger and moderator Luis Bilbao, an Argentine writer.

Bottom: Closing day of exchange. Speaking, writer Amiri Baraka. Others, left to right, are meditation teacher Dada Maheshvarananda; researcher Steve Brouwer; moderator Iván Padilla, Venezuela's deputy minister of culture for human development; and poet Amina Baraka.

Is socialist revolution in the US possible?

BY MARY-ALICE WATERS

FIRST, I WANT TO THANK the National Book Center, CENAL, and the organizers of the 2007 Venezuela Book Fair for their choice of the theme for this event. "The United States: A Possible Revolution" opens discussion on a question whose answer, in practice, will ultimately determine the future of humanity—or more accurately perhaps, whether there *is* a future for humanity.

I am speaking here today as one of a small minority, even among those who call themselves leftists, or revolutionaries, a minority that says without hesitation or qualification: Yes, revolution *is* possible in the United States. Socialist revolution. To put it in class terms, a proletarian revolution—the broadest, most inclusive social upheaval of the oppressed and exploited imaginable, and the rebuilding of economic and social relations in their interests.

As it deepens, that mass revolutionary struggle will win the support of the *majority* of the working class, small farm-

---

This was the opening presentation to the November 10–14, 2007, panel debate on the theme "The United States: A Possible Revolution," at the Third Venezuela International Book Fair.

ers, and other exploited producers and their powerful allies among oppressed nationalities, women, and others. It will be led by an increasingly class-conscious, tested, disciplined, and expanding political vanguard of the working class.

In the third American revolution, workers who are African American will be a disproportionately large component of the vanguard fighters and their leadership.

That revolutionary struggle will take political and military power from the class that today holds it. It will mobilize the strength and solidarity—the humanity—of working people in the United States on the side of the oppressed and exploited worldwide.

It will be a struggle that transforms the men and women who carry it forward as they fight to transform the twisted social relations inherited from the dog-eat-dog world of capitalism—relations that corrode human solidarity and coarsen us all.

What's more, revolutionary *struggle* by the toilers along the path I just described is *inevitable*. It will be initiated at first not by the toilers, but forced upon us by the crisis-driven assaults of the propertied classes. And our struggles will be intertwined, as always, with the resistance and struggles of other oppressed and exploited producers around the globe.

What is *not* inevitable, however, is the outcome of these coming revolutionary struggles. That is where political clarity, organization, prior experience, discipline, and the caliber of proletarian leadership become decisive. That is why what we do *now*, while there is still time to prepare, weighs so heavily. What kind of nucleus of what kind of revolutionary organization are we building today? What program, what continuity, guides its trajectory?

I wanted to assert this framework at the start so our discussion over the days to come can share a common vocabulary. This is the meaningful *class* content of the oft-abused word "revolution."

'Cuba and the Coming American Revolution'

One of the books being presented at this festival by Monte Ávila, one of Venezuela's leading publishers, bears the title *Cuba and the Coming American Revolution*. It was written by Jack Barnes, National Secretary of the Socialist Workers Party, and first published by Pathfinder Press in 2001. I mention it at the outset not just to salute the editors of Monte Ávila for their political perspicacity, and perhaps audacity, in publishing this new, 2007 edition of the book. More importantly, I want to introduce the book's theme as a part of our discussion.

Cuba and the Coming American Revolution is not primarily about the Cuban Revolution that triumphed on January 1, 1959—although it *is* about the worldwide impact of that revolution. As the back cover notes, it is, above all, "about the struggles of working people in the imperialist heartland, the youth who are attracted to them, and the example set by the people of Cuba that revolution is not only necessary, it can be made.

"It is about the class struggle in the United States, where the revolutionary capacities of workers and farmers are today as utterly discounted by the ruling powers as were those of the Cuban toilers. And just as wrongly."

The book highlights a statement made by Cuban leader Fidel Castro nearly five decades ago, on the eve of the US-organized invasion of Cuba at the Bay of Pigs.[1]

---

1. On April 17, 1961, 1,500 Cuban-born mercenaries, organized and

That abortive April 1961 assault was undoubtedly impe-rialism's greatest miscalculation in the history of our hemi-sphere, a blunder born of colossal class arrogance and class blindness on the part of those who considered themselves to be the rightful owners of all the wealth that the land and the toilers of Cuba together produced. That miscalcu-lation ended at Playa Girón in the glory of the first military defeat of Washington in the Americas.

A month before, in March 1961, Fidel told a cheering crowd of Cuban workers, farmers, and youth, "There will be a victorious revolution in the United States before a vic-torious counterrevolution in Cuba."

At the time, many of us on both sides of the Florida Straits knew that statement was not empty bravado, nor was Fi-del gazing in a crystal ball. He was speaking as a leader offering—*advancing*—a line of struggle for our lifetimes. He was addressing the question "What is to be done?"—both in Cuba and in the United States.

Each succeeding generation of revolutionaries in North America—and Cuba as well—has made those words our banner, with the determination to speed the day they will be fully realized.

Today, that flag is being held high by five Cuban revo-lutionaries now in their tenth year of imprisonment in the United States, where they are being held hostage by the US government as one more way to try to punish the peo-

---

armed by Washington, invaded Cuba at the Bay of Pigs on the south-ern coast. The invaders were defeated in less than seventy-two hours by the militia and revolutionary armed forces and police. On April 19 the last invaders surrendered at Playa Girón (Girón Beach), which is the name Cubans use to designate the battle.

"The Cuban Revolution that triumphed January 1, 1959, set an example that revolution is not only necessary, it can be made." It had a powerful and lasting impact on a generation of workers and students in the US deeply involved in the mass struggle against Jim Crow segregation.

Top: Detroit, Michigan, April 1961: Picket line called by Fair Play for Cuba Committee condemns invasion of Cuba at the Bay of Pigs by 1,500 Cuban-born mercenaries organized and armed by Washington.

Bottom: Victorious Cuban combatants celebrate defeat of the counterrevolutionary invaders in less than seventy-two hours.

GRANNA

RAMÓN ESPINOSA/AP

"For half a century the working people of Cuba have held at bay the most powerful empire history has ever known. Today their fighting determination is seen in the five Cuban revolutionaries held hostage in US prisons by Washington to punish the Cuban people for their refusal to surrender."

Top: Cuban militia women prepare to defend the revolution against threatened US military assault during October 1962 "missile" crisis.

Bottom: Gerardo Hernández, Fernando González, Antonio Guerrero, René Gonzáles, and Ramón Labañino—known worldwide as the Cuban Five—in Havana, December 2014, a few days after the final three—Hernández, Guerrero, and Labañino—won their freedom.

ple of Cuba for their refusal to surrender.[2]

The new edition of *Cuba and the Coming American Revolution* is dedicated to them. To "Gerardo, Ramón, Antonio, Fernando, and René—five exemplary products of the Cuban Revolution who today, even if against their will, serve with honor on the front lines of the class struggle in the United States."

Our deliberations and our actions here this week will advance the fight for their freedom.

A capitalist world free of crises?

Today, above all I want to address my remarks, with all due respect, to those who doubt that socialist revolution in the United States is possible—to those who believe, or fear, that US imperialism is too powerful, and that revolution has become at best a utopian dream.

---

2. In September 1998 the Clinton administration announced with great fanfare that a "Cuban spy network" had been uncovered in Florida and the FBI had arrested ten of its members. In June 2001, the five defendants put on trial—Fernando González, René González, Antonio Guerrero, Gerardo Hernández, and Ramón Labañino—were each convicted of "conspiracy to act as an unregistered foreign agent." Guerrero, Hernández, and Labañino were also convicted of "conspiracy to commit espionage," and Hernández of "conspiracy to commit murder." Sentences ranged from fifteen years to a double life term plus fifteen years for Hernández. The five revolutionaries—each of them today a "Hero of the Republic of Cuba"—had accepted assignments to keep the Cuban government informed about counterrevolutionary groups in the United States planning terrorist attacks against Cuba. Untiring efforts by the Cuban government and a broad international campaign demanding their release finally won the freedom of the last three—Hernández, Labañino and Guerrero—on December 17, 2014. On the same day, Presidents Raúl Castro and Barak Obama announced the restoration of diplomatic relations between the two countries, severed by Washington some fifty-five years earlier.

To those who harbor such doubts, I will pose a question:

What assumptions about the future, explicit or implicit, could justify such a conclusion? What would the future have to look like?

I hope others here will address this as well. But I would like to give my answer.

To reach that conclusion, you would have to believe that there won't again be economic, financial, and social crises, or devastating world wars, on the order of those that marked the first half of the twentieth century. That the ruling families of the imperialist world and their economic wizards have found a way to "manage" capitalism so as to preclude shattering financial crises and breakdowns of production and trade that could lead to something akin to the Great Depression. That they can put a stop to growing assaults on the economic, social, and political rights of the toilers; to spreading imperialist wars; to the rise of fascist movements that take to the streets.

You would have to believe that such a crisis of the capitalist system, if it did develop, would no longer be met by working-class resistance and the rise of a broad social movement such as exploded in the United States in the 1930s. That powerful proletarian upsurge, with class-struggle leadership, built mass industrial trade unions for the first time in American history.[3]

You would have to be convinced that competition among

---

3. A vivid description of the capitalist social crisis of the 1930s and a case study of the working-class response with class-struggle leadership can be found in the four-volume series by Farrell Dobbs: *Teamster Rebellion, Teamster Power, Teamster Politics,* and *Teamster Bureaucracy,* published by Pathfinder.

"To conclude that socialist revolution in the US is not possible, you'd have to believe that the ruling families have found a way to 'manage' capitalism so there won't again be world-shaking economic, financial, or social crises."

Above: Employees flee the New York headquarters of Bear Stearns, March 14, 2008, the day the fifth-largest US investment bank collapsed. Within six months, the failure of other top imperialist banks and insurance companies in the US and Europe confirmed not only the worst capitalist financial crisis since the 1930s, but at its roots a deep and accelerating worldwide contraction of industrial production, trade and hiring. **Inset:** Millions of workers and their families lost their jobs and homes as the crisis deepened.

REUTERS

SANTIAGO LYON: REUTERS/BETTMAN

"The opening guns of World War III were sounded in 1991, with the first Iraq War. We are living through the opening stages of what will be many decades of bloody imperialist wars."

Top: Taloqan, Afghanistan, May 2011. Protest demands halt to bombings by US-led forces. The night before four civilians—two men and two women—had been killed by air strikes there in what is already the longest war in US history.

Bottom: Aftermath of US bombing of the road from Kuwait City to Basra, Iraq, February 1991. In a slaughter that ranks as one of the great atrocities of modern warfare, US-led allied forces bombed, strafed, and shelled civilians and soldiers fleeing on foot or trapped in gridlocked vehicles. One US officer boastfully called it a "turkey shoot."

imperialist rivals, as well as between them and the more economically advanced semicolonial powers, is diminishing, not sharpening. That the stronger "Third World" countries can enter the ranks of the "First World" powers. That superimperialist illusions such as "a united Europe" are leading to a future of social harmony, peace, and prosperity for all countries and classes concerned.

You would have to believe that US imperialism *won* the Cold War, that it is an ascending not declining power, able to sustain indefinitely the financial, economic, and military dominance it established over "friend" and foe alike by the end of World War II.

Most important, you would have to believe that world capitalism's profit rates, which have been on a long downward curve since the mid-1970s, are now going to begin to rise for several decades at an accelerated pace. That we're on the eve of a sustained upswing of capitalist investment that will increase industrial capacity and hiring, as it narrows what are now growing divisions among working people as well as a widening gap between city and countryside.

You would have to believe the rulers can accomplish such a turnaround in the rate of capital accumulation while avoiding the massive destruction of productive capacity—human and physical—that was the product of decades of wars such as those that culminated in the imperialist slaughter of World War II.

The evidence is overwhelming that the future we face is the opposite.

Just read this week's headlines! Think about what is happening from Wall Street to Pakistan, from Moscow to Tehran, from the Shanghai stock exchange to the ever-deeper gold mines of South Africa, to the capitalist banks and their world financial system.

The opening guns of World War III were sounded a decade and a half ago already, with the first Iraq War, as Washington began to act on the pretense it had emerged as the victor in the Cold War. We are already living through the opening stages of what will be many decades of bloody wars like those in Iraq, Afghanistan, and then Iraq again. That is what the "transformation" of Washington's nuclear-armed military structure and strategy is all about.

What is coming are years of economic and financial crises of which the current, still-expanding "subprime mortgage crisis" in the US—and the even more massive debt balloon it is part of, on and off the balance sheets—offers only a hint.

What is coming are years that will bring increasingly organized resistance by a growing vanguard of working people pushed to the wall by the bosses' drive to cut wages and increase what they call productivity. And it is through those battles that the vanguard's consciousness of itself, as well as confidence and leadership capacity, will develop unevenly but apace.

What is coming are years of economic, social, and political crises and intensifying class struggle that *will* end in World War III, inevitably, *if* the only class that is capable of doing so, the working class, fails to take state power—and thus the power to wage war—out of the hands of the imperialist rulers.

A fighting working-class vanguard

In the United States, the outlines of these coming battles can already be seen. The historic shift is not ahead of us, it has already begun.

The most important political actions in the United States are ones you rarely see images of on your TV screen or read about in the press. Their power has been demonstrated, however, by the millions of workers who took to the streets on May Day the last two years in cities and towns large and small across the breadth of the country. That historic working-class holiday is being reborn in the United States as a day of *struggle*.

There have been strikes and organizing battles in factories and workplaces from California to Iowa, from Georgia to Utah. Working people, immigrant and US-born, Black, Latino, and Caucasian, have stood shoulder to shoulder—sometimes in the streets, sometimes inside their factories, and sometimes in front of their neighbors' homes—in face of raids by immigration cops picking off individuals for deportation or on criminal charges of "identity theft." The purpose has been to intimidate not only immigrants, but in fact all workers.

The workers who are helping each other hide from *la migra* in factories, and taking in each other's children when their parents are picked up, are not immigrants alone.

This working-class vanguard, which is small relative to the size of the working class as a whole, doesn't come out of the blue. It has developed in response to the employers' quarter-century-long antilabor offensive driving down wages and all social benefits, imposing literally life-threatening production speeds, and denying simple dignity to working people on and off the job.

Part of this offensive has been the bosses' oft-times organized efforts to secure themselves an expanding supply of undocumented workers—low-paid and nonunion—simultaneously filling their labor needs and providing a wedge to

"The workers who are helping each other hide from *la migra* in factories, and taking in each others' children when their parents are picked up, are not immigrants alone. A working-class vanguard, immigrant and US-born, Black, Latino, and Caucasian, has stood shoulder to shoulder."

Above: Workers' families confront immigration agents after raid on Swift meat processing plant in Greeley, Colorado, December 2006. More than 250 workers were separated from their families and loaded onto planes, with 75 of them deported to Mexico that same day and the rest imprisoned in Texas.

use in attempting to further divide and stratify the working class. To make each individual worker feel alone and isolated, not part of a powerful and purposeful class.

This is not to paint a rose-colored picture of the class struggle in the United States. My aim is not to convince you that the working class is on the offensive or anything close to that.

To the contrary, it is the employing class that remains on the offensive. Most labor battles end in defeats or, at best, standoffs. The unions organize a declining percentage of those working in the United States and their officialdom increasingly enters into political collaboration with the bosses. This has been demonstrated once again in the last weeks by the wretched agreements negotiated with the auto industry giants, freeing the employers from responsibility for retirees' future health care needs and capitulating to the bosses' demands for a substantially lower wage scale for new hires working side by side with current employees *doing the very same jobs.*

It's no wonder that today in the US only some 7 percent of workers in private industry are unionized—down from nearly a third of the private work force half a century ago. And it is going lower.

But none of this is new.

What *is* new, what *is* changing, what *is* of historic importance, is the shifting character, composition, and dynamics of the US working class. This is the biggest problem the US rulers face. It is ultimately a bigger crisis for them than their Iraq or Afghanistan wars—because it is more enduring.

The capitalist rulers can, and at some point will, temporarily pull back from any single front in their "global

"The US working class is being strengthened by its increasingly international character. Traditions of struggle by workers around the world are being added to traditions of working-class battles in the United States itself."

April 10, 2006: 500,000 people march in Washington, DC, on National Day of Action for Immigrant Justice. More than a million joined demonstrations that day across the US. On May Day, three weeks later, more than two million workers stayed off the job and poured into the streets in over 140 cities and towns in the United States, as that historic working-class holiday began to be reborn as a day of struggle.

war on terrorism." They can and will make adjustments in their relations with their European rivals, and negotiate tradeoffs with Russia or China. They still have plenty of room to maneuver.

But the working class in the United States, including its immigrant component—some twelve million of whom today carry documents not accepted by the cops and courts—is something else. The working class and other exploited toilers are the source of the capitalists' surplus value, which in turn is the source of their profits, wealth, social status, and state power. They utterly depend on this massive pool of exploited and superexploited labor. They cannot compete worldwide and accumulate capital without it—and increasingly, even with it.

That fact underlies the greater confidence, combativity, and politicization of layers within the broad working-class movement in the US today.

The battle to win the labor movement and the big majority of working people to defend the rights of immigrants is inseparable from the battle to organize the working class as a whole and rebuild the trade unions. For that reason, it has become one of the most important "domestic" political questions in the United States today. Right now, it is one of the greatest obstacles to taking even baby steps toward independent working-class political action and the transformation of the unions into instruments of conscious class struggle.

And it *is* a battle. Many workers—Caucasian, Black, Asian, Latino, all—are influenced by the virulent anti-immigrant campaign of sections of the ruling class. It is an issue that is determining the future of the labor movement and will continue to do so—much like the fight against Jim Crow segregation did in the 1950s and 1960s, and as the ongoing fight against all forms of racism and discrimination still does.

One of the most crucial fronts of this battle, it should be emphasized, is within the Black community, where the divide-and-rule strategies of the rulers find an echo—despite the fact that life experience and historical memory prepare the vast majority of African-American workers to be natural allies of those fighting for immigrant rights.

The bosses' divide and conquer strategy deeply affects immigrant workers, as well. It often serves to foster deep distrust and racial prejudice toward US-born workers, Caucasian as well as Black.

Workers in the United States, wherever they were born, face the same class enemy, and determined struggles on any front tend to pull workers together in face of the attempts to divide us. That is what is beginning to happen.

It was shown, among other things, by the massive, national, Black-led march on Jena, Louisiana, in September 2007 by some 20,000 demonstrators—Black, Caucasian, Latino and more, native-born and immigrant—protesting the unjust treatment meted out by the courts to six Black teenagers in that town. It was the first national action of its size and character in decades in the United States. The march on Jena was a good example of the ways in which the strengthening of a broader proletarian vanguard has already been registered, and it was undoubtedly nourished by the power of the recent May Day mobilizations and related actions.

Young Latino workers proudly participating in that action were learning firsthand, and for the first time, of the history of struggles by working people in the United States against Black oppression. And the enthusiastic welcome extended to them by their fellow marchers had a powerful impact on all.

The attempts of the employers to turn immigrant workers—among others—into scapegoats in order to guarantee the availability of a pool of superexploited labor will not cease. Any sharp economic crisis will intensify the battle for the political soul of the working class on this and other questions.

In previous periods of US history the rulers were successful in dividing working people along lines of race and national origin, as in the aftermath of the defeat of Radical Reconstruction following the Civil War, and during the wave of bourgeois reaction and anti-Black "race riots" after World War I. Today, however, it is precisely the unprecedented internationalization of labor, the vast scope of working-class migration, dwarfing the great waves of the nineteenth and early twentieth centuries, that is today one of our greatest strengths.

We learn from the traditions of struggle coming together from all parts of the world. As we fight shoulder to shoulder, it becomes harder for the bosses to pit "us" against "them." It becomes more possible to see that our class interests are not the same as those of "our" bosses, "our" government, or "our" two parties. In fact those parties and their government are *not* "ours," and we are *not* a single "we."

Revolutionary continuity

As decades of deepening crises and intensifying class struggle open ahead of us, we have something else in our favor. The revolutionary potential of the great radicalization in the 1930s was squandered and diverted into support for capitalism's "New Deal" and then its inevitable successor, the "War Deal"—culminating in the worldwide imperialist slaughter of World War II.

It was the resources and attraction of a powerful bu-

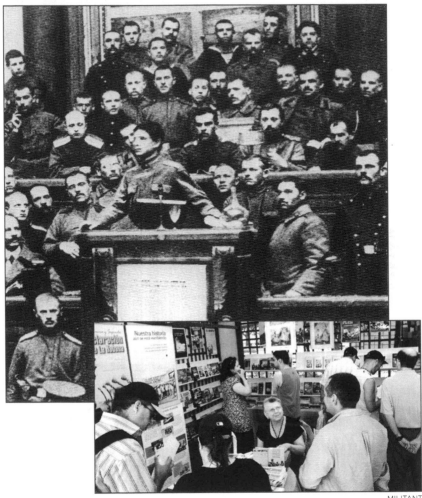

"As working-class battles deepen, the real history of the Cuban Revolution and Russian Revolution under Lenin will be sought after as new generations look to examples to learn how to fight to win."

Top: Soldier speaks to a council ("soviet") of soldiers and sailors during 1917 Russian Revolution. In October 1917 the working class, led by the Bolshevik Party, overthrew the regime of the capitalists and landlords, and the soviets of workers, peasants, and soldiers became the new government.

Bottom: Books and pamphlets recording lessons of more than 150 years of revolutionary working-class struggle worldwide were available at the Pathfinder booth at Venezuela book fair, November 2007.

reaucratic social caste in the USSR camouflaging itself as a communist leadership on a world scale that made this possible. Today, however, that enormous political obstacle no longer stands across the road toward independent working-class political action and revolutionary socialist leadership. Imperialism can no longer rely on it as an enforcer of peaceful coexistence, of "spheres of influence" around the globe. And the most combative and courageous leaders of working-class battles, of national liberation movements, of radicalizing youth, will no longer be drawn toward that Stalinist negation of everything Marx and Engels and Lenin fought for, falsely believing it to be communism.

That is why, as these battles politically deepen, the real history of the Cuban Revolution will again be increasingly sought after as new generations of vanguard fighters seek historical experiences from which they can learn not only how to fight but how to fight *to win*.

The lessons of the Russian Revolution and the Communist International under Lenin too will once again be studied.

Why has the Cuban Revolution traveled a completely different road the last twenty years, salvaging and fortifying its socialist revolution, as the bureaucratic regimes of Eastern Europe and the Soviet Union—which many falsely thought Cuba resembled—imploded?

How has it been possible for the Cuban people to hold at bay the most powerful empire history has ever known—or ever will know—for some fifty years?

Why to this day, despite decades of struggle throughout the hemisphere, does Cuba remain the only free territory of the Americas?

To state that fact is not to diminish the importance of the

space that has been conquered by the people of Venezuela these last years, nor the new ground still being taken in struggle. It simply registers the indisputable fact that what will be Venezuela's equivalent of the mass insurrection of the toilers of Cuba that culminated in the January 1, 1959, revolutionary triumph lies ahead of us, not behind. The Playa Girón of the Venezuelan toilers lies ahead of us, not behind.

It is in search of answers to these burning questions that even today books such as *The First and Second Declarations of Havana* and *Our History Is Still Being Written: The Story of Three Chinese-Cuban Generals in the Cuban Revolution*, are read worldwide with such great interest.[4]

Yes, socialist revolution is possible. It can be defended. It can be advanced even in face of our most powerful enemies. As the Cuban people have proven in practice, a better world is indeed possible. But in any radical or enduring manner, only through socialist revolution.

The stakes

The stakes posed in the questions we are discussing here at this event are immeasurable. We confront not only the destruction of the health, welfare, and environment of the earth and all toiling humanity—the destruction of land and labor, the wellsprings of all human progress and cul-

---

4. Meetings at the 2007 fair presented *Cuba and the Coming American Revolution* by Jack Barnes, *The First and Second Declarations of Havana*, *Malcolm X Talks to Young People*, and two books by Thomas Sankara: *We Are Heirs of the World's Revolutions* and *Women's Liberation and the African Freedom Struggle*. *Our History Is Still Being Written* was presented at the 2006 Venezuela book fair. These and hundreds of other Pathfinder titles in Spanish, English, and other languages were available to participants in the Caracas event.

ture. Those are and will be the inevitable, devastating consequences of the workings of capitalism. The limits we can impose on those consequences are and can only be a by-product of our revolutionary struggle.

Should the working class and its allies fail to take power out of the hands of today's capitalist rulers, however, we can be sure that we all face something else as well: an even more devastating future in the aftermath of the use of nuclear weapons.

Every revolutionary struggle, anywhere in the world—not least important right here in Venezuela—is a vital piece of the international battle. But until power is taken from Washington's hands by workers and farmers in the US, and Yankee imperialism is thus decisively disarmed, nothing lasting is settled.

That is why it is no small matter to answer: Yes, socialist revolution is not only possible in the United States, it is coming.

Yes, revolutionary struggles are on the agenda—but their outcome depends on us.

And yes, fighting shoulder to shoulder with others determined to triumph along this course is the most meaningful life possible

'The class battles ahead are inevitable, their outcome is not. That depends on us.'

BY MARY-ALICE WATERS

FIRST, A THANK YOU to all the panelists for their remarks—to José [González] from the ALBA Cultural Fund, Erick [Rangel] from the national leadership team of the United Socialist Party of Venezuela youth, and Carolina [Álvarez], editorial director of Monte Ávila.

On behalf of Pathfinder Press, I above all want to express our appreciation to Monte Ávila for the decision—described by Carolina—to publish *Is Socialist Revolution in the US Possible?* in not one but two editions for the 2008 Venezuela International Book Fair. One edition to be distributed without charge to book fair participants here tomorrow, and the other to be sold across the country over the coming year through the Librerías del Sur chain of bookstores.

One year after the Caracas book fair debate on "The United States: A Possible Revolution," Waters gave the following talk at the Fourth Venezuela International Book Fair. She was speaking as part of a panel launching a Spanish-language edition of *Is Socialist Revolution in the US Possible?* released that week by the Venezuelan publisher Monte Ávila. The November 14, 2008, presentation was jointly sponsored by Monte Ávila and Pathfinder Press.

I also want to thank the National Book Center, CENAL, the organizer of the Venezuela International Book Fair, for the important initiative its national leadership took last year in organizing the fair's rolling five-day debate on the theme, "The United States: A Possible Revolution." As you have already learned, that was the origin of the talk that is at the center of the book Pathfinder and Monte Ávila are jointly presenting here.

It is not by accident that the *New York Times*, the US daily newspaper most influential in molding bourgeois and petty-bourgeois opinion, just this week disparagingly singled out that event by name as an example of how divorced from reality all of us here in Venezuela are. How divorced from reality all revolutionary-minded workers are, everywhere. That we should even think such a ridiculous proposition worth discussing! That we should think events like the Venezuela International Book Fair, which promote reading and culture and civil debate among working people, point a way forward for humanity.

As we said last year, however, the question of whether socialist revolution is possible in the United States is no small matter. Its "answer, in practice, will ultimately determine the future of humanity—or more accurately, perhaps, whether there is a future for humanity."

A way to 'manage' capitalism?

What most struck me in rereading last year's presentation was the list of assumptions one would have to make to reach the conclusion that socialist revolution in the US is *not* possible. And then thinking about what has begun to transpire in the world in just the last twelve months!

"To reach that conclusion," we said, "you would have to

cuento "El caballero" el Primer Premio en el Concurso Anual de Cuentos convocado por el diario El Nacional de Caracas. Su novela: Los hijos, obtuvo el Segundo Premio Latinoamericano "Casa de Las Américas"- (Caracas, 1962). En cuento: Llegada de todos los trenes del mundo (Cuenca, 1932).

Mary-Alice Waters ¿Es posible una revolución socialista en Estados Unidos?

MICHAEL BAUMANN/MILITANT

MICHAEL BAUMANN/MILITANT

"The class battles ahead of us are inevitable, but their outcome is not. That depends on us. On our capacity to face the truth and speak with clarity to fellow combatants, to learn to rely on our own class solidarity and unity in struggle."

Top: Panel at Nov. 2008 presentation of *Is Socialist Revolution in the US Possible?* **Left to right:** Erick Rangel, youth leader of United Socialist Party of Venezuela; Mary-Alice Waters; Carolina Álvarez, editorial director of Monte Ávila publishing house; and José González, president of ALBA Cultural Fund.

Inset: Cover of Monte Ávila edition distributed at book fair.

Bottom: A lively discussion followed the presentations.

believe that there won't again be economic, financial, and social crises, or devastating world wars, on the order of those that marked the first half of the twentieth century. That the ruling families of the imperialist world and their economic wizards have found a way to 'manage' capitalism so as to preclude shattering financial crises and breakdowns of production and trade that could lead to something akin to the Great Depression. . . .

"You would have to be convinced that competition among imperialist rivals, as well as between them and the more economically advanced semicolonial powers, is diminishing not sharpening. . . .

"Most important, you would have to believe that capitalism's profit rates, which have been on a long downward curve since the mid-1970s, are now going to begin to rise for several decades at an accelerated pace."

In other words, you would have to think that the imperialist epoch with its inevitable conflicts, described by Lenin nearly a century ago, has been superseded by something new.

A year ago when we were discussing these questions here in Caracas, the main US stock market index, just a few weeks earlier, had closed at its all-time high of a little over 14,000. Yesterday it swung wildly by almost a thousand points, from under 8,000—more than 40 percent below that peak—to close at almost 9,000. These manic fluctuations have become so much a daily occurrence as to become commonplace. And everyone knows they simply announce another plunge.

The US Federal Reserve has lowered its ovenight interest rate to banks from nearly 5 percent to below 1 percent—in twelve weeks! Trillions of dollars of what Marx called "fictitious capital" have been "lost" in the last year—and so have the very non-fictitious homes and savings of millions of working people. Yet the bottom is not in sight.

The financial panic of banking capital is the symptom, however, not the disease.

What seemingly started as a capitalist crisis centered in credit and banking has now shown itself to be something of a different dimension. Its roots lie in the extended decline of the rate of accumulation of capital, the devastating contraction of new investment in plant, equipment, and hiring. As the de facto bankruptcy of General Motors bears witness, the deepest contraction of industrial production and employment since the opening decades of the last century has accelerated dramatically. Some two million workers have been thrown out of work in the US since the beginning of this year—already the greatest annual loss since the end of World War II.

The inevitability of such a contraction has underlaid this worldwide crisis from the beginning.

It is worth reminding ourselves that the Great Depression of the 1930s was not the consequence of the stock market crash of 1929 and subsequent banking crises alone. Its deeper origins are found in the violently intensifying competition among capitalist powers in the years leading up to World War I—competition for colonial possessions, access to markets and raw materials, and inexpensive sources of labor to exploit—and the economic and social breakdowns and financial catastrophe that accompanied that first interimperialist slaughter and its aftermath.

It took the global carnage of the Second World War, which included massive physical destruction across Europe and Asia from 1939 to 1945—and, above all, the postwar military, economic, and financial dominance of US imperialism—to lay the basis for the exploiting classes to pull out of that crisis. They did so first in the US and Canada, and then slowly across devastated Europe.

That is important. As Lenin stressed, there is no hopeless situation for capitalism. The two decades from 1930 to 1950 showed once again that the dons of finance capital, if they are not replaced beforehand by the workers and rural toilers, can dig themselves out of any crisis—by inflicting enough bloody defeats on the working classes and taking over enough of the world's destroyed industrial capacity.

The only question is the price the toilers will be made to pay.

And the only solution remains taking the power to inflict these horrors—state power—out of their hands, once and for all.

The road forced upon us

Is that possible? That is, after all, the question we posed a year ago. And we made the point that revolutionary struggles by the toilers are not only inevitable, they will be initiated at first not by us "but forced upon us by the crisis-driven assaults of the propertied classes."

The working class in massive numbers never enters on the road of revolutionary struggle lightly, or all at once. Workers sense the stakes, the sacrifices it will entail, the uncertainty. Our class in its majority exhausts other alternatives first, including the leadership of organizations looked to by large numbers of workers that are alternatives to communist political leadership.

Earlier this month tens of millions of workers in the United States cast their ballots for Barack Obama, the pres-

Monthly change in nonfarm
employment, 2004–2008

400,000

200,000

0

-200,000

-400,000

-600,000

2004   '05   '06   '07   '08

"Revolutionary struggle by the toilers will be forced upon us by the crisis-driven assaults of the propertied rulers."

Top: Unemployed workers line up outside job fair in New York City, November 2008.

Inset: More than two million workers were thrown into the ranks of the unemployed in 2008–09.

Bottom: Some 1,500 people of many nationalities joined July 2008 march and rally against immigration raid at Agriprocessors meatpacking plant in Postville, Iowa. Protest was led by women workers (one of them with bullhorn) displaying electronic ankle "bracelets" they were forced to wear by federal immigration cops.

idential candidate of one of the two dominant imperialist parties of the mightiest empire ever. One must be blind to history to think that the chief executive-elect of what Marx and Engels called the "committee for managing the common affairs of the whole bourgeoisie" can, or wants to, or will be allowed to do anything contrary to the interests of the propertied rulers who cold-bloodedly selected him as the best man for the job right now.

Even before the new stage of the global retrenchment we are now in the midst of, however, we have already seen, already been part of, the opening skirmishes of a fighting vanguard of the working class in the United States. We could see this vanguard-in-becoming as millions of workers took to the streets of cities and towns across the country in 2006 and 2007 asserting "we are workers not criminals," and affirming the dignity and combativity of some twelve million immigrants whose documents the US government does not recognize. Declaring "no human being is illegal," they retook last May 1 as a fighting holiday of the working class.

We could see the future earlier this year too, in the defiant response of workers across the Midwest—both immigrant and US-born—to raids by immigration cops on factories and homes, to the roundups and deportation of thousands of workers, to the criminal charges of "identity theft" brought against hundreds. The fighting response was captured most dramatically by the women, together with their children, who led the protest marches, proudly displaying the electronic police "bracelets" shackled around their ankles. It was registered by the workers of all nationalities who joined them.

These are the baby steps of a working-class vanguard

strengthened by its increasingly international character, by the traditions of struggle being added by workers from around the world to the longtime traditions of working-class battles in the United States itself. This is a working class that is slowly but surely learning in struggle the life-or-death necessity of fighting shoulder to shoulder—and how to do so.

The rapidly escalating economic and social crisis has only begun to be felt by working people, whether in the United States or internationally. While home foreclosures have been climbing over the past year—they will reach more than one million in 2008 alone—it is only in the last months that the factory closings and layoffs have begun to accelerate.

Just last week the DHL courier service shut down domestic service in North America, a move that will result in the layoff of more than seven thousand workers in the industrial belt of southern Ohio, with spreading repercussions for working people from Cincinnati to Dayton to Columbus. This year General Motors and other automobile companies have pushed thousands onto the streets, and thousands more auto and auto parts workers all over the country, and indeed all over the world, will follow in the months ahead—regardless of whether or not GM or Chrysler or both file for bankruptcy in the near future. Yahoo, the internet company, is laying off 10 percent of its workforce worldwide. Monster banks are slashing their workforces. And you can multiply those examples manyfold.

The majority—both in the United States and beyond, including here in Venezuela—still live with the grim hope that maybe the slump really won't get so bad, perhaps its worst possibilities will bypass our lands. But one thing is certain: as history teaches, world capitalism in crisis will not spare the most vulnerable.

A fight for political clarity

I want to close by emphasizing one point.

Our job today is above all a political one. While the class battles ahead of us are inevitable, their outcome is not. That depends on us. On our capacity to unflinchingly face the truth and speak with clarity to fellow combatants, to learn to rely on our own class solidarity and unity in struggle. To understand, and help other vanguard fighters to understand, that the driving force of all history since the dawn of recorded time has been class struggle, not conspiracies. That the poisons of racism, race-baiting, and Jew-hatred rob us of our ability to see that the real problem is the capitalist system itself, and that the real enemy we must defeat is the propertied classes whose wealth and power depend on that system.

Working people the world over are in for decades of intertwined economic, military, social, and political crises, and accompanying explosive class battles. The period we are entering will be more akin to the years from the opening of the twentieth century through World War II than to anything any of us have lived through. The one thing we can be sure of is that our side, our class, will have more than one opportunity to alter the course of history in the only way we can—the way the workers and farmers of Cuba did it fifty years ago, and the way the working people of the tsarist empire did it four decades before them.

That's why the continuing example of the Cuban Revolution is so important today. And, I would add, it's why the fight to free the five heroes of the Cuban Revolution—

who, against their will and ours, have been serving on the front lines of the class struggle in the United States for more than ten years now—is an international battle of the first order.

All these are among the real questions in front of us. For the opportunity to address them, and to join in the debate over them, both this year and last, we express our thanks, our respect, and our class solidarity.

MILITANT

FILVEN

"The book fair was marked by the resources the Venezuelan government is devoting to the expansion of literacy and popular access to culture."

Top: Dance performance at 2007 Venezuela International Book Fair.

Bottom: Fairgoers browse titles by Venezuelan publishers in main tent.

Prospects for revolution in the US
A necessary debate among working people

BY OLYMPIA NEWTON

I

CARACAS, Venezuela—The first two days of the November 9–18 Third Venezuela International Book Fair have been marked by the expansion of literacy and popular access to culture in this country, as well as political debate sparked by the fair's theme, "The United States: A Possible Revolution."

A wide variety of books are for sale—from poetry collections to histories of the struggles against Spanish colonial rule in South America, from cookbooks to titles on the place of the Cuban Revolution in the world today. Nearly eight hundred book presentations and artists' performances offer a place for working people and others to discuss literature, the arts, and politics. Almost two hundred publishing houses are participating.

These articles reporting on the forum "The United States: A Possible Revolution" appeared in the November 26 and December 3, 2007, issues of the *Militant*, a socialist newsweekly. The full text of the opening presentation by Waters was published in the December 17 issue.

"The rebirth of culture being celebrated here is especially significant considering all the books and bookstores that were burned during the years of the dictatorships in our countries," Alicia Castro, Argentina's ambassador to Venezuela, said at the opening ceremony. She was referring to the brutal military regimes that dominated much of Latin America during parts of the 1960s, '70s and '80s. Argentina, which from 1976 to 1983 endured one of the most murderous of those tyrannies, is the country of honor at this year's fair.

Reflecting the Venezuelan government's programs to preserve the languages and cultures of indigenous peoples, the inaugural ceremony was kicked off by a children's choir that sang the national anthem in the language of the Anu people. Minister of Culture Francisco Sesto and Vice President Jorge Rodríguez were the featured speakers. Rodríguez described the expansion of publishing and book distribution in Venezuela in recent years, and the literacy campaign that has taught more than one million workers and peasants to read and write.

'United States: A Possible Revolution'

Ramón Medero, president of the National Book Center (CENAL), welcomed participation in the fair by many individuals active in a variety of social movements, especially those coming from the United States. He also introduced the fair's theme, "The United States: A Possible Revolution." Noting that the fair's central activity is a five-day rolling forum on that topic, Medero pointed to the importance of the fact that participants will be discussing "not just whether a revolution is necessary in North America, but that it is possible."

The week-long discussion featured twenty-two panelists, mostly political activists and writers from the United States, as well as a number of US citizens living in Venezuela.[1] Four or five of them spoke each day, debating diverse political views. Hundreds of Venezuelans and others took part in one or more sessions, with dozens asking questions and making comments from the floor. The event was covered by Venezuelan television, radio, and newspapers. The issues debated on the character of the working class and prospects for revolution in the United States sparked a political discussion that permeated the book fair.

The debate's opening session, attended by one hundred fifty people, was November 10. The panelists at the morning session were Mary-Alice Waters, a member of the Socialist Workers Party National Committee and president of Pathfinder Press, and Eva Golinger, a Venezuelan American lawyer and journalist, author of *The Chávez Code* and *Bush vs. Chávez*.

The afternoon panelists were US-born journalist

1. In addition to panelists mentioned in this account, others included Charles Hardy, a former Maryknoll priest who has lived in Venezuela for many years; University of Minnesota political science professor August Nimtz; former University of Colorado professor Ward Churchill; Dada Maheshvarananda, a US-born Hindu meditation teacher living and working in Caracas; and William Blum, a writer on the history of CIA operations.

Some speakers invited to take part in the forum were unable to make it during that event, but joined the discussion in the following days. A November 17 program featured Kathleen Cleaver, former national spokesperson for the Black Panther Party. A video interview with Noam Chomsky, the linguistics professor, anarchist, and author, was played after the conclusion of the forum, and a booklet containing a translation of his comments was distributed.

Chris Carlson, a regular contributor to the website venezuelaanalysis.com, and Tufara Waller, coordinator of the cultural program of the Highlander Center in Tennessee and director of the We Shall Overcome project. Their remarks and the subsequent discussion from the floor opened a debate on several of the most sharply contested issues.

"I am speaking here today as one of a small minority, even among those who call themselves leftists, or revolutionaries, a minority that says without hesitation or qualification: Yes, revolution *is* possible in the United States. Socialist revolution," said Waters, the opening speaker. "What's more, revolutionary *struggle* by the toilers along the path I just described is *inevitable*. It will be initiated at first not by the toilers, but forced upon us by the crisis-driven assaults of the propertied classes."

Waters said she was addressing those who consider socialist revolution in the United States to be impossible, "a utopian dream." Such a conclusion, she said, has to rest on the assumption "that there won't again be economic, financial, or social crises, or devastating wars, on the order of those that marked the first half of the twentieth century."

"You would have to be convinced that competition among imperialist rivals, as well as between them and the more economically advanced semicolonial powers, is diminishing not sharpening. . . .

"Most important, you would have to believe that world capitalism's profit rates, which have been on a long downward curve since the mid-1970s, are now going to begin to rise for several decades at an accelerated pace," she said. "That they can accomplish such a turnaround in the rate of capital accumulation while avoiding the massive destruc-

JACOB PERASSO/MILITANT

"The battle to win the labor movement and the big majority of working people to defend the rights of immigrants is one of the most important 'domestic' political questions in the United States today. It will determine the future of the labor movement."

Top: May 1, 2007, march in Chicago of 150,000 demanding end to raids and deportations.

Bottom: September 2007 protest of 20,000 in Jena, Louisiana, condemns biased court ruling against six African American youth. The welcome given by participating immigrant workers from Central America dealt a blow to prejudice used by the bosses to divide and weaken the working-class movement.

tion of productive capacity—human and physical—that was the product of decades of wars such as those that culminated in the imperialist slaughter of World War II."

Developing working-class vanguard

The economic crisis of capitalism drives the bosses' offensive against the working class in the United States, Waters said, and these assaults are generating resistance. She pointed to the mass street mobilizations on May Day the last two years demanding an end to factory raids and deportations by *la migra*, and the scapegoating of undocumented immigrants as evidence of the beginning development of a working-class vanguard.

She said the mobilization last September of tens of thousands against racist injustice at the hands of the cops and courts in Jena, Louisiana, was "the first national action of its size and character in decades" and "was undoubtedly nourished by the power of the recent May Day mobilizations."

In this context, Waters said, "The real history of the Cuban Revolution will be sought after once again," as will the lessons of the Russian Revolution and the Communist International under Lenin, "as new generations of vanguard fighters search for historical experiences from which they can learn not only how to fight but how to fight *to win*."

"How has it been possible," she said, "for the Cuban people to hold at bay the most powerful empire history has ever known—or ever will know—for some fifty years? Why to this day, despite decades of struggle throughout the Americas, does Cuba remain the only free territory of the Americas?"

In her remarks Golinger said, "I have to disagree that Cuba is the only free territory of the Americas. Because here in Venezuela we are also free." She predicted that the

government-supported package of constitutional amendments will pass in a December 2 referendum here despite a
campaign by the proimperialist opposition, and pointed to
this as an example of how "we are freeing ourselves with
the enemy living in the same house."[2]

Golinger also said she didn't "share the same optimism
that a revolution is possible in the United States." Golinger,
who has lived in Venezuela since 1999, said that in prepar-
ing for the book fair she had spoken "with Noam Chomsky
about how the process of change will have to be very slow
in such a capitalist consumer society as the US."

People in the United States are deadened to conditions of
suffering, Golinger said, because "it's very easy to change the
channel. People are not poor or hungry in the US like they were
in Venezuela. There is poverty but only in a few small sectors.
You get two or three credit cards in the mail every day."

As for the movement demanding an end to raids and
the deportation of immigrants, Golinger said, "Even though
they were demanding to be recognized, what they want is
to live inside a capitalist consumer society."

"The only way to achieve structural change in the United
States is to make advances here" in Venezuela, she said.
"Then we can go there and say, 'Look at the Bolivarian Rev-
olution, what we've accomplished. You can do the same.'"

Issues are joined

The two presentations were followed by a lively discussion,
and the issues presented on the opening day have been hotly

---

2. The December 2, 2007, referendum on a package of sixty-nine constitutional amendments was defeated by a 51–49 percent margin, with
a high abstention rate.

FILVEN

MILITANT

FILVEN

"The stakes posed in the questions we are discussing are immeasurable. Until power is taken from Washington's hands by the workers and farmers and Yankee imperialism is decisively disarmed, nothing lasting is settled."

Panelists and audience joined the issues during the five-day exchange on "The United States: A Possible Revolution."

Top: Participant speaks from floor. At speakers' table, from left: former Maryknoll priest Charles Hardy; Bernardo Alvarez Herrera, Venezuela's ambassador to US; moderator José González, president of the ALBA Cultural Fund; University of Minnesota professor August Nimtz.

Bottom left: Tufara Waller, director of cultural program at Highlander Center in Tennessee.

Bottom right: Chris Carlson, US journalist living in Venezuela; Luis Bilbao, moderator.

contested at other book fair activities, too. Golinger's remarks reflect widely held opinions here that there is little
hope for revolutionary change in the United States.

The majority of those speaking during the first round
of discussion at the event expressed doubts at such a possibility. Several Venezuelan speakers said in various ways
that living standards in the United States are too high for
there to be working-class resistance, or that people are
brainwashed by capitalist-owned media.

Some participants from the United States offered a different view. "I don't consider myself to have been turned into
an idiot," said Diógenes Abreu, a Dominican-born activist
living in New York. "Nor do I consider the millions who live
in the United States who oppose its policies to be idiots.

"But I also don't share all the optimism of Mary-Alice,"
Abreu said. "If, as she pointed out, only some 7 percent
of private-sector workers are organized, and the working
class has to be in the leadership of a revolution, how can
you say it's possible sooner rather than later?"

"The people I work with have never read Noam Chomsky,"
said Tufara Waller from the Highlander Center in Tennessee. Pointing to working people in New Orleans still confronting the social disaster in the wake of Hurricane Katrina,
as well as tobacco farmers in North Carolina fighting to
keep their land, she noted, "They are people who are hungry, who understand that they have to fight to live." And
many people in the United States don't have credit cards,
either, Waller added.

Two-party system

The discussion continued in the afternoon, kicked off by
Waller and Chris Carlson. Originally from Colorado, Carl-

son has lived in Venezuela for the last three years. "Many Venezuelans, including President Chávez, say that Bush is the problem," he said. "But Bush is not the problem. He is just a product of a system dominated by big corporations." Carlson's presentation documented the fact that both the Democratic and Republican parties in the United States are financed by the same major corporations.

Contenders for the Democratic and Republican party nominations for the 2008 presidential elections, he said, present fundamentally the same perspectives: driving ahead with the war in Iraq, and maintaining the economic embargo against Cuba and hostility toward Venezuela. The candidates are now debating health care, he said, but none has any proposal other than to keep health care a money-making institution at the expense of the well-being of millions.

Waller described the history of the Highlander Center and its current projects to organize against environmental degradation, intolerable working conditions, and racist discrimination.

"If both parties are so dominated by the monopolies, why don't people rise up against them?" a Venezuelan participant asked Carlson. Referring to the idea often heard in left-wing circles in the United States that the 2000 election was stolen from Democratic Party candidate Al Gore by supporters of George W. Bush in Florida, Carlson said the majority of people in the United States don't see it that way and "consider the Bush administration a legitimate government."

A young Venezuelan who just returned after living in the United States also took the floor during the discussion. He described the school he attended in a working-class area of Alabama. "The education system there is not about learning at all," he said. The young people he went to school with wanted to change society but didn't know how to begin. "This forum is only the beginning of what will be several days of discussion on these themes," said program moderator Luis Bilbao, an Argentine-born journalist, at the conclusion of the first day.

II

Among the issues discussed at the five-day forum, the sharpest debate focused, first, on the impact and importance of millions of Latin American immigrant workers in the United States. And, second, on the history of revolutionary struggles of working people in the United States and the lessons of those struggles for revolutionary perspectives. In a striking way, the discussion registered that those living and engaged in the class struggle in the United States generally expressed greater confidence in the revolutionary capacities of working people there than did those— both US citizens and Latin American participants—living outside the United States.

Several panelists are active in work to expand rights for immigrants in the United States. These included Diógenes Abreu, the Dominican-born community organizer who currently lives in New York; Luis Rodríguez, a Chicano activist in California's San Fernando Valley; and Gustavo Torres, an organizer for the immigrant rights group Casa de Maryland. Several of them gave vivid and concrete pictures of conditions of life for immigrant workers in the United States and the growing resistance and confidence manifested in strikes and ongoing street mobilizations against raids and deportations.

Both Torres and Antonio González, president of the Southwest Voter Education and Registration Project, said the road to "empowerment" is organizing Latinos to vote. "What does a revolutionary do in the US today?" asked González. "Take power wherever you can" by electing Latinos to city, state, and federal offices. The graphs he projected for all to see depicted the growing number of Latino voters and officeholders.

During the discussion periods day after day, a number of participants from Venezuela and elsewhere in Latin America took exception to the evidence that immigrant workers resisting the superexploitation they face in the United States are an important part of the working-class vanguard that is emerging there. In various ways, several said that Latin Americans living and working in the United States are simply there to get "a piece of the pie."

"They are only out there to get passports," said one participant. "Once they get them they'll stop marching." Many spoke with barely concealed contempt for immigrant workers as sellouts who have bought into the "American dream" instead of remaining in Latin America to fight for political, economic, and social change.

In the discussion, Carlos Samaniego, originally from Paraguay and today a meat packinghouse worker in Minnesota, countered this view. He described the vanguard role that immigrant workers are playing in struggles in the United States—from coal mines in the West to union struggles in Midwest slaughterhouses.

America's revolutionary heritage

The other hotly debated question was the revolutionary history of toilers in the United States and, by extension, prospects for a third American revolution, a socialist revolution.

"America was created by revolution," said panelist Lee Sustar, labor editor of the *Socialist Worker* newspaper, which reflects the views of the International Socialist Organization. Speaking at the November 13 session, he referred to the US Civil War as "the completion of the bourgeois-democratic revolution" that had won independence for the thirteen British colonies some eighty years earlier.

"There has never been a revolution in the United States, and anyone who thinks there has been is ignorant of their own history," responded British journalist Richard Gott, a former editor at the *Guardian* in London. Gott said the American Revolution, which defeated British colonial rule, could not be considered a revolution. Rather, it was a war to take land from Native American tribes, whose territory, he said, was being protected against the American colonists by the British royal army.

"No, a revolution is not possible in the United States," said Gott. "It is conservative and reactionary. The only hope is Latin America."

"I want to express my total agreement," interjected Haiman El Troudi, the Venezuelan moderator of the panel that day. "There never has been a revolution in the United States and never will be!" El Troudi has held several offices in the Chávez government and written books including *Being Capitalist Is Bad Business* and *History of the Bolivarian Revolution*.

"It is impossible for a revolution to begin in the United States," said a Venezuelan participant from the floor. He pointed to what he considered US workers' complicity with Washington's wars against Iraq and Afghanistan as proof that working people there are desensitized to injustice.

"There has never been a revolution in the United States and never will be!" asserted one panelist. The revolutionary history of toilers in the US and prospects for a third American revolution, a socialist revolution, were hotly debated at Caracas forum.

Top: Black troops, most of them freed slaves, during the Civil War of 1861–65, the second American revolution. Some 200,000 served in Union Army.

Bottom: Blacks confronting counterrevolutionary mob, as pictured in July 1868 *Harper's Weekly.* Person at center depicts official of Freedmen's Bureau, established in 1865 and initially headed by a Union Army general.

Postwar Radical Reconstruction governments in the South implemented laws barring race discrimination, establishing free public schools and clinics, taxes on large landholders, universal male suffrage, expanded rights for women, and public relief. Militias organized defense against counterrevolutionary assaults. Social conquests were products of struggle by toilers of all skin colors, often led by former slaves.

But in remarks during the November 11 panel, ex-Marine and founder of Iraq Veterans Against the War Jimmy Massey described his own evolution from a prowar patriot to a staunch opponent of the war in Iraq. He walked through day-to-day experiences in Iraq that led him to oppose US policies in the Middle East and to organize fellow soldiers to do the same.

Another idea frequently expressed by speakers from the floor and by a few panelists was that "change has to come from the South," referring primarily to Latin America. Many said the only hope was to wait until enough countries in Latin America close their doors to imperialist penetration so as to cause a collapse in the US economy. The fact that nowhere in Latin America but Cuba have working people yet successfully carried through to victory the kind of revolutionary struggle necessary to end imperialist domination was largely absent from that picture.

Some participants argued that US capitalism would be thrown into crisis if enough "leftist" governments were elected in Latin America and refused to sign bilateral "free-trade" agreements with Washington or join the US-initiated Free Trade Area of the Americas. Others pointed to popular struggles in Venezuela, Ecuador, Bolivia, and Nicaragua as being the key to educating working people in the United States. Despite different arguments and emphases, the point of agreement was that no initiative could be expected from working people inside the imperialist bastion.

A contrasting point of view was presented by Héctor Pesquera, a leader of the Hostosiano Independence Movement of Puerto Rico. "The Puerto Rican struggle is connected to the North American revolution," he said. Pesquera summarized the worsening conditions facing both working people in Puerto Rico and Puerto Ricans living in New York. Pointing to the movement that forced Washington to withdraw its naval base from the Puerto Rican island of Vieques, Pesquera noted that this blow to the US rulers had strengthened social movements in the United States.

"I'm going to take issue with what every one of you has said," stated Amiri Baraka, a writer from Newark, New Jersey, speaking from the audience during one of the sessions. Baraka, who later spoke as a panelist, has been active in Black nationalist, Maoist, and Democratic Party politics since the 1960s. He attacked Sustar for not identifying himself as a "Trotskyite," and falsely accused panelist George Katsiaficas of having introduced himself as a former member of the Black Panthers (he hadn't done so). Baraka's intervention was the first time in four days of sharp debate that the tone of civil discourse was breached.

Final session

"When I first heard the theme of this forum, I thought it was a joke," said Steve Brouwer, an American living in Venezuela and writing a book on peasant cooperatives. Brouwer was a panelist at the final session. "But the more I thought about what is happening in the world, the more I listened to my Latino brothers here, the more I became convinced that revolutionary change in the US *is* possible."

Brouwer said that working-class complacency in the United States in the 1920s had given way to labor battles in the 1930s that shaped US politics for forty-five years. He cited a "mildly progressive" Democratic Party, influenced by these developments in the labor movement, as key to what he called a progressive course that ended with the election of Ronald Reagan in 1980.

Amina Baraka, also a panelist at the final session, introduced herself as "a Black woman who is a communist who uses the cultural arena." She spoke about her work and read a poem.

Amiri Baraka came back to the previous day's discussion, disagreeing with Gott and others who denied there have been two great revolutions in US history. He also disagreed with Sustar's characterization of the Civil War as the completion of the bourgeois-democratic revolution that began with the independence struggle of the colonies.

"That revolution has never been completed," Baraka said. "There is still no democracy for Blacks." He proposed that Blacks and Latinos, including a layer of the Black bourgeoisie, unite around a program to abolish the electoral college; establish a unicameral parliamentary system; ban "private money" from election campaigns; make voting compulsory; and restore voting rights to felons. Such constitutional reforms, he said, would shift power toward "people's democracy" in the United States. Revolutionary goals could then be put on the agenda.

What has derailed all previous revolutionary struggles in the United States, Baraka argued, is "white privilege." He cited the defeat of Radical Reconstruction following the Civil War, the failure of the 1930s labor upsurge to go further, and the decline of the mass movement that brought down Jim Crow segregation as three examples. Moreover, "white privilege," and the failure of the "white left" to fight it, remain the primary obstacle to struggles today.

Baraka also renewed his attack on Katsiaficas, who as part of the panel the previous day had spoken about Asian student struggles. Baraka accused him of being an agent who had selected that topic in order to try to stir up support in Venezuela for student marches against the government of Hugo Chávez.

Baraka concluded by reading "Somebody Blew Up America," a Spanish translation of which was distributed to participants. Written by Baraka after September 11, 2001, the verse presents a long list of historical atrocities, interlacing anti-imperialist and anticapitalist rhetoric with conspiracy theories of history and anti-Semitism. "Who decide Jesus get crucified," the poem asks. "Who knew the World Trade Center was gonna get bombed / Who told 4000 Israeli workers at the Twin Towers / To stay home that day / Why did Sharon stay away?"

During the opening day of the panel, a participant from Panama had said during the discussion that Jews are the main problem facing working people in the world today because "they have all the money" and control everything. Norton Sandler, a member of the Socialist Workers Party in the United States, spoke from the floor the next day and pointed to the deadly danger scapegoating and Jew-hatred posed for the working-class movement.

After Baraka's remarks the final day, Mary-Alice Waters took the floor to thank the organizers of the book fair "for bringing together diverse forces with such a broad variety of views for the discussion that took place here." She stressed the importance of civil debate, noting that "the poison of agent- and race-baiting must be condemned by all."

At the close of the five-day forum, Ramón Medero, president of Venezuela's National Book Center, the sponsor of the fair, expressed his appreciation to all the panelists whose efforts had contributed to the success of the event, and satisfaction that the fair served to open a much-needed political discussion.

INDEX

Abreu, Diógenes, 73, 75
Afghanistan war, 10, 40, 43, 77
Africa, 10, 39
Agent-baiting, 22, 81–82
Álvarez, Carolina, 8, 53
American Revolution, First
(1775–83), 11, 23, 77
American Revolution, Second
(1861–65)
See Civil War, US
Anti-Semitism
See Jew hatred
Argentina, 66
Asia, 10
Auto industry, 43, 61

Baraka, Amina, 81
Baraka, Amiri, 23–26
agent-baiting by, 22, 80–82
on Jews and conspiracies, 12,
21–22, 82
on parliamentary reform, 26
on race-baiting and "white skin
privilege," 12, 19–20, 22, 81
on US Civil War and Radical
Reconstruction, 81
Barnes, Jack, 15, 31
Bay of Pigs, 31–32, 50
Being Capitalist Is Bad Business
(El Troudi), 77
Bilbao, Luis, 75
Blacks, 24, 26, 81

and strengthening of working-
class vanguard, 45–46
in third American revolution, 30
Blum, William, 67
Bolivia, 79
Brouwer, Steve, 80
Bush, George W., 74
Bush vs. Chávez (Golinger), 67

Capitalism
as danger to human survival,
40, 50–51
depression of 1930s, 36, 57, 70
dog-eat-dog values of, 30
and immigrant labor, 41–43, 45
and interimperialist rivalries,
36–39, 40, 45, 57, 68
no hopeless situation for, 58
and offensive against working
class, 17–18, 36, 41–45, 68–70
postwar expansion of, 36
prospects for "managing," 36–
39, 54–56, 68–70
sharpening crisis of, 9–12, 19,
36–40, 57–58, 61–62, 68–70
sows divisions among toilers,
19, 21, 40, 46–47
Capitalist crisis, post 2007
financial panic: symptom, not
disease, 57
household income, decline in, 10
interest rates, decline of, 56–57
investment in plant and
equipment, decline of, 57

mortgage crisis in US (2007–08), 40, 56–57
profit rates, decline of, 39, 56, 68
unemployment, 10, 19, 57, 61
Carlson, Chris, 68, 73–74
Castro, Alicia, 66
Castro, Fidel, 31–32
CENAL (National Book Center, Venezuela), 15, 29, 54, 66
Chávez Code, The (Golinger), 67
Chávez, Hugo, 22, 74
China, 45
Chomsky, Noam, 67, 71, 73
Churchill, Ward, 67
Civil debate, 16, 22, 80, 82
Civil rights movement, 46
Civil War, US (1861–65), 11, 23, 77, and Radical Reconstruction, 47, 81
Class collaboration, 43
Cleaver, Kathleen, 67
Cold War, 39–40
Communist International, 49, 70
Communist Manifesto, 21
Conspiracy theories, 21–22, 82
Constitution, US
amendments won in battle as "flash points" today, 24
Amiri Baraka on parliamentary reform, 26
Cuba and the Coming American Revolution (Barnes), 15, 31, 35
Cuban Five, 32–35, 62–63
Cuban Revolution
US and, 32–35, 74
and Venezuela, 50
world example of, 31–32, 49–50, 62–63, 70
Culture and literacy, 50, 54, 65–66

Democratic Party, 19–20, 60, 74, 80
DHL layoffs (2008), 61
Dobbs, Farrell, 36

Ecuador, 79
El Troudi, Haiman, 77
Engels, Frederick, 21, 49, 60
European Union, illusions in, 10, 39

Farmers, 29, 31, 51, 73
Fascism, 36
Fictitious capital, 56
First and Second Declarations of Havana, The, 50
Free Trade Area of the Americas, 79

General Motors, 57, 61
Germany, 22
Golinger, Eva, 18, 67, 70–73
Venezuela, not Cuba, shows way forward, 26
González, Antonio, 76
González, Fernando, 35
González, José, 53
González, René, 35
Gore, Al, 74
Gott, Richard, 26, 77, 81
on American Revolution as "landgrab" from Native Americans, 23
Guardian (London), 77
Guerrero, Antonio, 35

Hardy, Charles, 67
Health care, 43, 50, 74
Hernández, Gerardo, 35
History of the Bolivarian Revolution (El Troudi), 77

Home foreclosures, 40, 56–57, 61

Hurricane Katrina, 73

Immigrant workers
attempts to scapegoat, 19, 40, 45–47
impact of, 45
as key question in US politics
capitalists' need for, 17, 41–43, 45
and emerging working-class vanguard, 16–17, 41–47, 75–76
growth of, 16–18, 45, 47
and strengthening of working class, 16–17, 43–45, 47
petty-bourgeois contempt for, 11, 18, 71–73, 76
raids and deportations against, 41, 60, 70–71, 75
superexploitation of, 41–43, 45, 76
as "workers, not criminals," 60
See also May Day actions, Working class and exploited toilers

International Socialist Organization, 23, 77

Iran, 39

Iraq war (2003–), 10, 40, 43, 74, 77–79

Jena, Louisiana, 46, 70

Jew-hatred, 21–22, 62, 82

Jim Crow, 45–46

Katsiaficas, George, 80–82

Labañino, Ramón, 35

Labor party, 17, 45

Latin America, 66
Cuba as only free territory in, 49–50, 70, 79
economic crisis in, 10
as "only hope" for revolution in Americas, 26, 77–79
See also Cuba, Venezuela

Lenin, V.I., 49, 56, 58, 70

Libya, 10

Maheshvarananda, Dada, 67

Malcolm X Talks to Young People, 50

Marx, Karl, 21, 49, 56, 60

Massey, Jimmy, 79

May Day actions, 17, 41, 46, 60, 70, 75

Medero, Ramón, 66

Militant (New York), 15–16, 65

Monte Ávila (publisher, Venezuela), 12–13, 15, 31, 53–54

"New Deal"/"War Deal," 20, 47

New Orleans, 73

New York Times, 54

Nicaragua, 79

Nimtz, August, 67

Obama, Barack, 58
on US economy "doing pretty darn well," 9

Our History Is Still Being Written (Waters, ed.), 50

Pakistan, 39

Pathfinder Press, 11, 15–16, 31, 36, 50, 53–54

Pesquera, Héctor, 79–80

Playa Girón
See Bay of Pigs

Puerto Rico, 79–80

Race-baiting, 20, 22, 62, 81–82

Racism, 19–20, 46, 62, 70, 74

Radical Reconstruction, 47, 81

Rangel, Erick, 53

Reagan, Ronald, 80

Republican Party, 60, 74

Revolution, socialist
  building leadership today for,
    16–17, 27, 30, 51, 62
  and communist continuity, 27,
    30, 47–49, 70
  inevitability of revolutionary
    struggle, 27, 30, 51, 58, 62,
    68–70
  necessity of, 9–11, 15, 29, 40,
    50–51, 54, 58
  possibility of in US, 19, 26–27,
    29–32, 35–36, 62, 68–70
  program, importance of, 27, 30
  and transformation of working
    people, 30

Rodríguez, Jorge, 66

Rodríguez, Luis, 75

Russia, 39, 45
  See also Soviet Union

Russian Revolution, 49, 70

Samaniego, Carlos, 76

Scapegoating, capitalist, 19, 21–
  22, 40, 47

Sesto, Francisco, 66

South Africa, 39

Soviet Union, 20, 49
  See also Russia

Stalinism, 20, 47–49

Stock market, 56–57

Sustar, Lee, 23, 77, 80

Syria, 10

Teamster series (Dobbs), 36

Terrorism, "global war on," 43–45

"Third World," 39, 79

Torres, Gustavo, 75–76

Ultrarightists, 36, 40

Unions, 17, 19–20, 36, 45, 76
  impact of immigrants on, 45,
    weakening of, 43

United Socialist Party of
  Venezuela (PSUV), 53

United States
  Bush's "stolen" 2000 election
    in, 74
  capitalist bipartisan setup, 58–
    60, 74, 80
  Communist Party,
    subordination of workers'
    struggles by, 20
  elections of 2008, 58–60, 74
  immigration to, 16–17, 41–43,
    45, 47
  and nuclear weapons, 40, 51
  presidential election (2016), 10
  revolutionary history and
    legacy, 23–26, 76–77
  revolutionary prospects in, 18–
    19, 26–27, 29–32, 35–36, 62–
    63, 68–70
  rulers' pretense they won Cold
    War, 39–40

Venezuela, 61, 74, 79
  fight for literacy and culture
    in, 66
  illusions within, 23, 70–71
  and working-class struggle for
    power, 49–51

Venezuela Book Fair (2007), 50,
  debate at, 11–13, 15, 22, 29,
    53–54, 65–82

Waller, Tufara, 68, 73–74

We Are Heirs of the World's
  Revolutions (Sankara), 50

Women, fight for rights by, 29–
  30, 60

Women's Liberation and the

African Freedom Struggle (Sankara), 50

Working class and exploited toilers
battles in 1930s that built unions, 19–20, 36, 47, 80–81
capitalist offensive against, 17, 36, 41–43, 45, 68
class interests of: not "our" bosses, "our" government, 47
confidence and combativity of, 41–43
countryside, gap with city, 39
divisions within, 39, 45
employers retain offensive, 43
and immigrants
campaign against by sections of ruling class, 45–46
defense of, stakes in organizing, 16–17, 41, 45–46
strengthening by, 16–17, 45, 47, 60–61
See also Immigrants
independent political action by, 17, 20, 45, 47

petty-bourgeois lack of confidence in, 11, 18, 24–26, 71–73, 77
resistance to bosses' attacks, 17, 20, 36, 40, 46, 62,68–70, 73
revolutionary potential of, 16–17, 22, 26–27, 29–31, 40, 58, 62, 75
as source of bosses' profits, wealth, power, 45
struggle to unify, 19, 46–47, 61
vanguard, emergence of, 17, 40–41, 46, 60, 70
See also Revolution, socialist

World War I, 57
and "race riots" against Blacks, 47

World War II, 36–39, 40, 57–58, 68–70
and Franklin Roosevelt's "War Deal," 20, 47

World War III, 40

Yahoo, layoffs by (2008), 61

ALSO BY MARY-ALICE WATERS

Cosmetics, Fashions, and the Exploitation of Women

Joseph Hansen, Evelyn Reed, Mary-Alice Waters

How big business plays on women's second-class status and economic insecurities to market cosmetics and rake in profits. And how the entry of millions of women into the workforce has irreversibly changed relations between women and men—for the better. $15. Also in Spanish and Farsi.

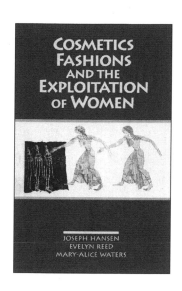

Che Guevara and the Imperialist Reality

Ernesto Che Guevara was among the most outstanding leaders forged by Cuba's socialist revolution. The internationalist course he helped lead strengthened not only the Cuban Revolution but the working class and its allies within the US itself. In a world still dominated by imperialism, Waters notes, the odds have shifted in favor of the oppressed and exploited. $6. Also in Spanish.

Rosa Luxemburg Speaks

Edited by Mary-Alice Waters

Rosa Luxemburg's place of honor among the great revolutionary Marxist leaders of the twentieth century has often been denied her. Here she speaks for herself, with clarity and wit, taking on political battles that continue to divide revolutionaries from reformists in the workers movement even a century after her murder in Berlin in 1919 by counterrevolutionary militias. $30

Is socialist revolution in the US possible?

Are They Rich Because They're Smart?
Class, Privilege, and Learning under Capitalism
Jack Barnes
"In the coming battles forced upon us by the capitalist rulers workers will begin to transform ourselves and our attitudes toward life, work, and each other. Only then will we discover our own worth and learn what we're capable of becoming." $10. Also in Spanish and French.

50 Years of Covert Operations in the US
Washington's Political Police and the American Working Class
Larry Seigle, Farrell Dobbs, Steve Clark
Traces the decades-long fight by class-conscious workers against efforts to expand presidential powers and build the "national security" state essential to maintaining capitalist rule. $12. Also in Spanish and Farsi.

"It's the Poor Who Face the Savagery of the US 'Justice' System"
The Cuban Five talk about their lives within the US working class
In a 2015 interview, five Cuban revolutionaries talk about their experiences as part of the US working class during their 16 years in US federal courts and prisons. And prospects for Cuba's socialist revolution today. Includes 24 pages of photos. $15. Also in Spanish and Farsi.

Cuba and the Coming American Revolution
Jack Barnes

A book about the struggles of working people in the imperialist heartland, the youth attracted to them, and the example set by the Cuban people that revolution is not only necessary—it can be made. It is about the class struggle in the US, where the political capacities and revolutionary potential of workers and farmers are today as utterly discounted by the ruling powers as were those of the Cuban toilers. And just as wrongly. $10. Also in Spanish, French, and Farsi.

Malcolm X, Black Liberation, and the Road to Workers Power
Jack Barnes

"Don't start with Blacks as an oppressed nationality. Start with the vanguard place of workers who are Black in broad proletarian-led struggles in the United States. The record is mind-boggling. It's the strength and resilience, not the oppression, that bowls you over."—*Jack Barnes*. $20. Also in Spanish, French, Arabic, Farsi, and Greek.

Teamster Politics
Farrell Dobbs

A central leader of the battles records how Minneapolis Teamster Local 544 combated FBI and other government frame-ups in the 1930s; organized the unemployed; mobilized labor opposition to US imperialism's entry into World War II; and fought to lead labor and its allies on an independent working-class political course. $19. Also in Spanish.

Revolutionary leaders

The Communist Manifesto
Karl Marx, Frederick Engels

Founding document of the modern revolutionary workers movement, published in 1848. Communism is not a set of preconceived principles imagined by would-be reformers but the line of march of the working class toward power—a line of march "springing from an existing class struggle, a historical movement going on under our very eyes." $5. Also in Spanish, French, Arabic, and Farsi.

Lenin's Final Fight
Speeches and Writings, 1922–23
V.I. Lenin

In 1922 and 1923, V.I. Lenin, central leader of the world's first socialist revolution, waged what was to be his last political battle—one that was lost following his death. At stake was whether that revolution, and the international movement it led, would remain on the proletarian course that had brought workers and peasants to power in October 1917. $20. Also in Spanish and Greek.

The Revolution Betrayed
What Is the Soviet Union and Where Is It Going?
Leon Trotsky

In 1917 workers and peasants of Russia were the motor force for one of the deepest revolutions in history. Yet within ten years a political counterrevolution by a privileged social layer whose chief spokesperson was Joseph Stalin was being consolidated. The classic study of the Soviet workers state and its degeneration. $20. Also in Spanish, French, Farsi, and Greek.

... in their own words

Cuba and Angola
Fighting for Africa's Freedom and Our Own
Fidel Castro, Raúl Castro, Nelson Mandela

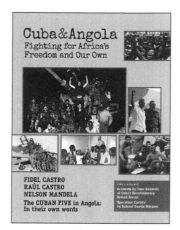

In March 1988, the army of South Africa's apartheid regime was dealt a crushing defeat by Cuban, Angolan, and Namibian combatants in Angola. Here leaders and participants tell the story of the 16-year-long internationalist mission that strengthened the Cuban Revolution as well. $12. Also in Spanish.

Malcolm X Talks to Young People

"The young generation of whites, Blacks, browns, whatever else there is—you're living at a time of revolution," Malcolm said in December 1964. "And I for one will join in with anyone, I don't care what color you are, as long as you want to change this miserable condition that exists on this earth." Four talks and an interview given to young people in the last months of Malcolm's life. $15. Also in Spanish, French, Farsi, and Greek.

Problems of Women's Liberation
Evelyn Reed

Explores the social and economic roots of women's oppression from prehistoric society to modern capitalism and points the road forward to emancipation. $15. Also in Farsi and Greek.

Puerto Rico: Independence Is a Necessity

Rafael Cancel Miranda

One of the five Puerto Rican Nationalists imprisoned by Washington for more than 25 years speaks out on the brutal reality of US colonial domination, the campaign to free Puerto Rican political prisoners, the example of Cuba's socialist revolution, and the ongoing struggle for independence. $6. Also in Spanish and Farsi.

Maurice Bishop Speaks

The Grenada Revolution and Its Overthrow, 1979–83

The triumph of the 1979 revolution in the Caribbean island of Grenada under the leadership of Maurice Bishop gave hope to millions throughout the Americas. Invaluable lessons from that workers and farmers government, defeated by a Stalinist-led coup in 1983. $25

We Are Heirs of the World's Revolutions

Speeches from the Burkina Faso Revolution, 1983–87

Thomas Sankara

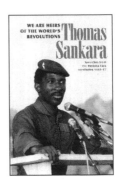

The peasants and workers of this West African country established a popular revolutionary government and began to fight the hunger, illiteracy, and economic backwardness imposed by imperialist domination, and the oppression of women inherited from millennia of class society. Five speeches by the leader of this revolution. $10. Also in Spanish, French, and Farsi.

Cuba's Socialist Revolution

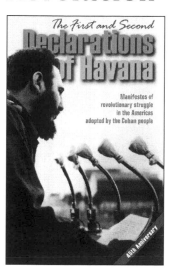

The First and Second Declarations of Havana

Nowhere are the questions of revolutionary strategy that today confront men and women on the front lines of struggles in the Americas addressed with greater truthfulness and clarity than in these uncompromising indictments of imperialist plunder and "the exploitation of man by man." Adopted by million-strong assemblies of the Cuban people in 1960 and 1962. $10. Also in Spanish, French, Arabic, Farsi, and Greek.

Our History Is Still Being Written

The story of three Chinese-Cuban generals in the Cuban Revolution

Armando Choy, Gustavo Chui, and Moisés Sío Wong talk about the historic importance of Chinese immigration to Cuba, and the place of Cubans of Chinese descent in more than five decades of revolutionary action and internationalism. $20. Also in Spanish, Farsi, and Chinese.

NEW INTERNATIONAL NO. 11

U.S. Imperialism Has Lost the Cold War
Jack Barnes

Contrary to imperialist expectations, with the collapse of regimes across Eastern Europe and the USSR claiming to be communist, the Cuban Revolution did not follow suit. Cuban working people and their leadership have continued to show the world what "socialist revolution" means. $16. Also in Spanish, French, Farsi, and Greek.

WWW.PATHFINDERPRESS.COM